All That Ricochets

Emily Arjune

BookLeaf Publishing

India | USA | UK

Presentation by *BookLeaf Publishing*

Web: www.bookleafpub.com

E-mail: info@bookleafpub.com

ISBN: 9789358315134

First edition 2023

For those who need to be reminded there is
light within them.

In another poem about Van Gogh

The poet wrote about his stars,
his night curled in lovers' breath,
constellations carried on the wind.
How he saw the world; one sweeping galaxy
reaching for another
above a trembling village

And I think that's what true love is
The tragedy of those soothing hands
The lonely space between our fingers
painting restless hope everywhere.

To everyone who cast their stones

My body is a deep riverbed
both swallowing and being swallowed

Palms are sacred underwater
unconditional deliverance from hell
Cupping good faith
and the chance
to be
renewed.

Blue

the shape of my longing
to kiss you in waves of amber,
my sweet whiskey mouth
breaks on your lips.
I pull away
as though my own feelings
have broken a rule
The question rolls on our tongues
like a marble
I don't ask
You don't answer
My skin cracks open
wounds and all
but it's you I wanted
to lick clean.

Layers

4

Healing is an undoing
an unfolding
an unwrapping
arms open
wrists exposed
layers peeling
hazardous in your old skin
that delightful singe
of feeling sunlight
for the first time.

Monuments

5

In this space
between war and whisper
Teeth and flesh
urgent
unyielding
where soft finds sharp
someone will find us
in the ruins of a
tight fist
buried in sunlight.

The day the sun was born

Kingdoms forged
pockets of wonder
tucked under linen skies
soft cotton cradle
named constellation.
I pray You
eat clouds with spoons,
sip moonlight punch
from a dragon's paw
and never forget
You are the Northern Lights
setting fire to the night
You are a fairytale
slaying monsters.

You are the universe
tracing galaxies
on my palm.
Faithful starlight
is your blanket
wrapped in the
endless breath
shared, softly bleating
chest to chest.

After Love

I slipped into devastation
like an old cardigan

A comfortable hazard
for my body to drip over

the couch like candle wax
what's left of the flame

softened, flayed to
the sun-bleached bone

And the cardigan
open, wearing itself

alive.

Dragonflies

8

The dragonflies danced overhead
while the grass below
wears my body like a birthmark.
Like I have always been there,
just faded
in wine-stained trouble
trying to remember a time
I wasn't trying to bury myself.
A time whenever I breathed
the little universe trembled
in prayer,
in mourning,
in a constant state of being loved.

Sated

In those faded midnights
when I became a morsel compass,
that is something infinite
to be tasted,
to be swallowed,
These bodies of ours
speak ancient tongues
Holy words
carved in the bedrock
of my skin
I am a prayer caught
in your throat
A torchlight on its last
flicker of life
humming
an electric
song.

Peach tree

There are days
when I am like a tree
ripe with regrets
falling from my mouth
like a rotten peach:
anger
jealousy
shame
All the unbeautiful
parts of me
slick; melted
syrup offering
the earth
what's left
of the sunset rind.
And the peach
now soil
now seed.
Perhaps the greatest mercy
I have earned is
the chance to rise again.

This one is for you

For always holding me gently
tender, cupping the river of me
in your palms
I used to think your touch
was fearful
like you were cradling a bomb
like I was a danger to time
Now I know
you held me bravely
the seabed of your body
giving my pain
a place to rest.

Anxiety is

12

the way time presses against me like an
ill-fitting shirt/constantly on the edge of
folding/buckling in the chasms of bruised
knuckles/always a first draft of
myself/rebuilding/relentless/reduced to
shards/the clock takes note of every second I run
nowhere/the unconquerable race/skinned knees
at the finish line/time is the jewel and death is
the thief/the coat is too big/swallowing
everything

Natural disasters or why I can't love gently

What a landslide I was
when I fell for you
I could stop breaking
on impact
This love
the ruin of a storm
that stripped house
from foundation
the ravenous earth
swallowing a village

I'm never just a spark
I burn the forest down.

Convalescence

The armor hangs by the hearth
left there when you did
its sleeves covered in rubble
from detonation.
The unfolding in me came
in a slow-burn romance with forgiveness.
A grenade on a water-lily --
the only thing separating calm
from disaster is time.
Just like grief, I wish to sheathed.
Put the weapon on the mantle.
My body softens in a new sweater
while the candles speak for me,
down the hall
peace waits for sleep.

She was

15

the winter ground
waiting to thaw
under stone soil
yielding no harvest.
The burrowing noise
of underground life
stirring warmth and
yearning through rubble
underfoot from beast.
A fawn stepping forward
seeing the sky
for the first time
velvet touching velvet.
Grey forgotten linen
hung to dry
over somber fields
clinging to the melt
trading seeds
for virtue from
the grave raven.
Alive,
a busy spring
but in no hurry.

I said I would marry you

But I die first. Keep my body wrapped in my favorite blanket when offering me back to the earth. My life belongs to anyone who speaks my name; the broken promise. I wrote my eulogy when we said our vows; preserved my bouquet for the coffin. Inevitable was my gown. Your spirit, my bone. This daughter of envy tricked by the roads not taken. To avoid perjury, the choir sings the crescent truth of my myth. Tip the bards with lavender and send them off with my favorite kind of chocolate as favors. Lean in. Kiss me through the shroud. I swear I will be smiling.

Willow

Grief does not leave
its shoes by the door

It enters dragging mud
across the floors

stirring the howl of a storm
in the kitchen

Soon, it leaves its
toothbrush overnight

strands of hair
trapped in the carpet

making a home
of your ribcage.

That specter waiting
at the end of the hall

A widow watching
the willow bend to the rain

The beast panting
on the doorstep

let it in to
nuzzle on your lap

It will slither to
the basement

to be forgotten.
Buried under the

hunching willow.

Ivy

The lattice of my fingers
climb like ivy
to the peaks of your timbers
stretching to the shudders
of your hands
begging to keep them
open and tangled
in my vines
of hair and sunlight
warming the stone
of your chest
You kiss me
invite me in
let me crawl
atop the mantle
of your mouth,
twisting over
clover and bedrock
until you're covered
in a peaceful slumber.
A quiet burial
for the morning dew.

All that ricochets

When I open, I rattle
picket fence eyelids shudder
hinges cracking like bones.
Thunder finds the bullets
kept warm behind
my eyes
until all I want is
to rake my fingers through
grass, churning green
into coffee
smash mugs on
the countertop
I am chalk bleeding
down the drive
while the gates
punch open from
the wind. Open,
close
open, close.

My Father's Daughter

I saw it once, your temper,
in the mirror
when I was cleaning
up casings of
a battle both won
and lost.
Its face void of regret
framed generations,
still relentless
behind glass.
So much the moon
to me; tides folding
and pillaging the shoreline
against ever
changing moods.

I found my baby book
where you'd called me
princess
the same weekend
you cursed a
bed frame for
slipping from your palms,
your study in
letting something fall
when it becomes too heavy.

I see the disappointment
greying our eyes.
Bristled attitudes paint
threats colors of neutral.
Blind to the space
between apologies
and surrender.
I cursed
the solider
the "old soul"
portrait of the
ancestor whose
spirit lives in my footprints.
Whose war never ended.

Closure

My trauma was there
in the photo albums
and camera rolls.

Hiking up the Grand Canyon
and spotted amongst
all the lights in Vegas.

It's the ones where I'm
smiling the brightest that
should be burned.

It lived in all the people
who should have been
my home.

Whose gallantry
only lived in the
flash of nighttime memory.

I give myself the grace
to know I had no choice
but to carry it.

And I'm not breaking
anyone's heart by letting it go.